RHYMES & JOKES
FOR LITTLE FOLKS

and big ones too.....

Lee Smith

ISBN: 0-75961-385-0

This book is printed on acid free paper.

All Rhymes and most art by Lee Smith with some help from
Dover Publications / Design Dynamics / Volk / Click Art / Graphic Products

1stBooks – rev. 9/13/01

Dedicated to Molly

SILLY STUFF

Write a Silly Poem of sing a Silly Song
Draw a fierce Grumpdoodledork 65 feet long.
Dance with a Giant Rabbit that no one else can see.
Be a great Magician or a silly Chimpanzee.

Hang upside down and watch the world go by
Imagine you can walk on the ceiling like a fly
Make a droll Hand Puppet that talks to little kids
Invent a game where everyone tells outrageous fibs.

Read a bold adventure book and dream what you can be
The pictures in your mind are better than TV
You're only a kid once so enjoy the Silly Stuff
There's lots of time for serious after you grow up.

PET DRAGON

If you buy a baby Dragon.. and keep him as a pet
You'll be surprised at all of the attention that he gets
Folks will feed him Fritos.. and want to pet his head
And it may be fun to sleep while he's curled up on your bed

But while he's growing up.. you may have second thoughts
Your food bill will quadruple with everthing you've bought
And the day will come when your house is way too small
And that cute little dragon is forty five feet tall !

BALLOON RIDE

Captain Hippo and the Flying Baboons
Went for a ride in a big balloon
Sailing high up toward the moon
Singing "Up, up and away!"…

They said "Let's fly East…no, let's fly West
Which way do you think is the best?"
But it didn't matter (as you probably guessed)
As the wind blew them all away….

A Baboon hollered.. "We're going too fast !
I fear this ride will be our last"
But Captain Hippo just chuckled and laughed
As the wind just blew and blew…

The wind blew them across the sea
To Spain and France and Italy
Where they landed in an olive tree
And sampled one or two…

"That was fun" said the Flying Baboons
Let's go back at half past noon
And take a lunch of cheese and prunes
In a brown paper sack..
And hope the wind blows us back."

BULLDOZER

I'd like to drive a Bulldozer
And doze a bull or two
If I found one dozing
That's what I would do
I'd pick him up and move him
While he slept peacefully
Way up to the top of our big maple tree

I'd scoop up great chunks of snow
To make a GREAT SNOWMAN
And folks would come from miles to see
My winter wonderland

Way up high.. to the sky
Like one big white mountain
And people with their sleds and skis
Would ski down my snowman.

PANDEMONIUM

There was pandemonium at the bakery
When they gave away Sticky Buns and Cookies were all FREE
The Cream Puffs and Doughnuts, Cakes and Custard Pies
Were all FREE too.. much to our surprise

People came from everywhere and jammed into the store
They grabbed and gobbled goodies and spilled them on the floor
The Baker called the riot squad to try to make 'em stop
But the Custard pies went <u>SPLAT</u> in the faces of the Cops !

ASTRONAUTS

We're going to the Moon today
Tomorrow we'll try Mars
We Astronauts are brave enough
To journey past the stars

We'll take peanut butter sandwiches
To last our trip through space
But we'll be back by suppertime
So it won't go to waste.

We'll probably meet Aliens
On planets yet unknown
Strange but friendly creatures
Like tiny elflike gnomes

Or maybe giant monsters
With scaly reptile skin
We'll show them that the Earthmen
Aren't afraid of them

At least I hope
We can.

MY ROBOT

I made a robot named KERPLINK to serve me every day
He has no brain, he has no heart and never disobeys
He's just parts assembled with wire, screws and glue
And I give him commands and tell him what to do.

When I spill something on the floor he cleans it up but then
He doesn't run and tell my Mom..with a silly grin
He even walks my dog, while the neighbors stare
They ask if they can rent him but I don't want to share.

He mows the lawn and does the chores that I'm supposed to do
And I don't have to pay him or even say "Thank you"
My invention brings attention everywhere I go
And scientists all marvel when KERPLINK shovels snow.

But one day my brother.. tinkered with KERPLINK
He put a brain inside his head and now the creature <u>thinks</u>
I said "KERPLINK, you're the slave and <u>I</u> am the master!"
And that was the recipe for next days disaster.

He marched outside the house and held a picket sign
Saying "I'm <u>not</u> a slave, for now I have a mind!"
The next day I woke to find KERPLINK had marched away
I heard he joined the service with a Tech Sergeants pay.

He now commands a squad of Special Force Machines
They're the Gung-Ho, chrome plated, bullet proof Marines.

TATTOO PARLOR

Benjamin Blue walked into
A Tattoo Parlor store
He said "I'll get one, just for fun
Just one and nothing more
An anchor on my arm like Popeye
That is all I want
But, wait…maybe my chest could use
A great big elephant !

Well, he liked that tattoo so much
He could not stop at that
So he added two Green Dragons
That covered all his back

Next came a dancing Elvis
And a long stretch Limousine..
While Hearts and Rosebud flowers
Filled all the space between

All the skin left over had colored polka dots
Done in good taste, of course
Not like Chicken Pox..
It cost $2000 for all those tattoo marks
Now he moonlights at carnivals
Showing off his art.

CLOWN

"Laugh and the world laughs with you"
Is the motto of a clown
He puts a smile on faces
Where once there was a frown
He's got jokes and tricks
That will leave you in stitches
And a Slapstick to whack
Other clowns in baggy britches.
The Circus tent is up
And they're coming to town
Those wild & crazy guys
The CLOWNS !

FLU BUG

Ruby had the flu bug...but she pass it on
To Genevieve and Harold who passed it on to John
And as the Preacher told us..(and this I believe)
"It's better, my friends, to give than to receive."

GIGGLES

Benny Bojangles Melancop
Got the giggles and could not stop
When he got tickled he giggled some more
And fell and rolled all over the floor
In fact he giggled right out the door
Down the street past the candy store
He rolled right down a big steep hill
And bumped into his good pal Bill
His pal Bill was so amused
He joined right in and they giggled in two's
It seemed contagious as the flu
So soon the whole town was giggling too
The last I heard they were giggling still
And that's the story of Benny and Bill.

REBECCA'S NOSE

Every time Rebecca lied
Her nose would grow and grow
Just a little, then a lot
Then a whole lot more

She lied to her Mother
She lied to her teacher
She told a fib about her trip to
Lands of Giant Creatures

Her nose grew so long that
She couldn't use a glass
She drank and dribbled from a straw
It was an awful mess

The birds all perched on her nose
Because of it's great size
And all because Rebecca
Told so many lies.

COUNT DRACULA

Count Dracula has Royal Blood
At least that's what they say
But when he bites you on the
neck
He'll take some away.

He has two long fangs
And a case of bad breath
And the mention of his name
Scares folks half to death.

He says "When the sun goes
down
I go out for a bite
And I might dine on you
If your windows aint locked
tight."

But the Count went to a Dentist
Who pulled out both his fangs
Saying "There's too many
cavities"
And the Count said "I'll be
danged !"

So no more blood for Dracula
To freshen up the dead
He'll have to be satisfied with
Tomato juice instead.

PIRATE SHIP

I sailed upon a Pirate Ship
With Blackbeard and his crew
A rowdier bunch of rascals
Never sailed the ocean blue
I wore a fake beard
With a patch above one eye
So they never suspected
I was not a Pirate guy
I climbed up in the crows nest
And shooed away the crows
I said "Land ahoy, Mateys"
And also "Thar she blows !"
A Pirate with a parrot
Brought his treasure chest outside
The parrot did the talking
As they divvied up the prize
He said "Let's take that little guy
And feed him to the sharks !"
Then my Mom said
"Wake up John…it's almost 8 oclock."

SINGING TELEGRAM

I'm sending my friend Jason
A Singing Telegram
I'll say "Will you be my Valentine
Signed your good friend Ann"
I'll sing the telegram myself
Just inside his fence
And I'll make the telegram collect
And charge him fifty cents.

SURFING THE NET

The exercise that I like best is surfing on the net.
What a way to stay in shape without getting wet
When I feel that urge.. to exercise come on
I lie down on the davenport until the feeling's gone.

RALPH THE WONDERDOG

My dog Ralph read "War and Peace"
Though it was quite a strain
But he prefers much simpler things
That do not tax his brain
That he reads at all is great
So we should not deplore
The weird newspapers that he buys
In Supermarket stores.

THE DENTIST

A wise old dentist from Boston
Said "If you have teeth please floss 'em
Don't be like the kid
Who lied "Yes, I did"
So they all went bad and he lost 'em.

BOMBS AWAY!

A little robbin flying by
Dropped some doo doo in my eye
It could have been worse, says I
I'm just glad that pigs don't fly.

DOCTOR GRAYBEARD

A doctor with a long gray beard
Said "It is just as I have feared
You've watched that TV screen non-stop
Now Televisionitis is what you've got
The only cure that I know
Is listening to the Radio
But you turn the sound up so high
You'll hurt your eardrums bye and bye
So if you can't listen and you can't look
May I suggest...read a book !

GROUNDHOG DAY

On February 2nd little Punxatawny Phil
Pops up from the ground like Groundhogs often will
If he sees his shadow there'll be six more weeks of cold
But if he don't there won't… that's what I've been told
Some folks think it's Silly, some say it's OK
But Groundhogs wouldn't have it any other way.

MOUNTAIN CLIMBER

Why do I climb mountains ?
Just because they're there
Instead of sitting comfortably
In my easy chair
Of course if there's an avalanche
Then I might worry
And come down the mountain
In a real big hurry !

A THREE DOG NIGHT

Where's the Concert.. where's the park ?
We don't have time to kill.
The Smashing Bumpkins open for
The Hounds of Baskerville.
The steering wheel is on the right
'Cause it's an English car
GANGWAY ! …everyone…
We're off to see the Stars !

ST. PATRICKS DAY

Leprechauns and pipers..flags and marching bands
Begorrah, it's a grand sight.. straight from Ireland
Come one..come all, we'll have a ball
So wear somethin' green
And join in the best parade that you have ever seen !

St. Patrick chased the snakes clear out of Ireland
So you won't be bothered here by the likes of them
But Shamrocks we have plenty and Corned Beef Cabbage Stew
And singers with high voices singing "Too ra loo rah loo"
"May the wind be at yer back" goes an Irish toast for thee
"But when you break wind, don't stand in front of me !"

DICKIE BIRD

A little yellow Dickie Bird hopped on my window sill
He chirped "Wake up you sleepyhead, it's almost quarter till"
He sang a song and banged upon my windowpane with glee
And I dreamed of a recipe for Dickie Fricasse.

ARE WE THERE YET ?

(Frere Jacques tune)

"Are we there yet..Are we there yet ?
Is it far ..in the car?"
"Settle down and sit there !
We'll tell you when we get there!
Take a nap..where's that map ?"

"Are we there yet..Are we there yet ?
Jenny and me..have to pee."
"We'll find a filling station
Somewhere close to Dayton
You'll have to wait..oops!..too late."

"Are we there yet..Are we there yet ?
Cant we stop..for some pop ?"
"There's O J in the cooler
Get your crayons and color !
Next time why..don't we fly?"

KING HENRY THE 8TH

Crosspatch, crosspatch..why are you so dour ?
Did Henry the 8th lock you in the Tower ?
Did you hide his crown or steal his doggies bone?
Did you put a whoopie cushion on his Royal Throne?
Violets are purple … roses are red
Here comes the Chopper to **chop off yer 'ead** !

THE DARE

"I'll give you a nickel if you go tickle that sleeping tigers feet"
That was a dare from my friend Bo to see how scared I'd be
So I sneaked up behind that cat and tickled both his feet
But he giggled, chuckled, wiggled and laughed
Instead of eating me.

OOPS!

I ate onion soup and cheese macaroni
Some pop and a pickle and a slice of baloney
OOPS ! I've got gas...and I'm turning purple
What will relieve it...maybe a burp'll.

THE CLONE

Harriet Barbara Wilma Jones
Thought she'd like to have a clone
She wished upon a Magic Lamp
And there she was… ALACAZAM !

Well, they looked so much like each other
No one could tell...not even her Mother
When Harriet started to comb her hair
Her clone did too, just like in a mirror

Whenever one spoke the other did too
And they stopped together as if on cue
Even their shadows stuck like glue
It was downright spooky I'm telling you
So said all their teachers...

Neither was stronger..neither was weaker
Birds of a feather in purple sneakers
Sounding like two stereo speakers
So Harriet got what she deserved
They got on everybodys nerves.

HAUNTED HOUSE

In this empty Haunted house are ghosts who walk at night
So says a neighbor who saw them ..one dark rainy night
He's 25 years old but his hair turned snowy white
Now he won't walk by the place unless it's broad daylight.

Poncho and I didn't believe in scary Ghosts and Spooks
So we sneaked inside one dark night and heard something go **BOO!**
The doors creaked, the shutters banged and much to our surprise
We saw a creature with **three yellow staring eyes!**
    YOW! ..our hair stood on end and we ran like the wind
        And you can bet we will never go in *there* again!

TRICK OR TREAT

Those horrible creatures the TRICK OR TREATERS
Are coming down the street
They're Monsters, Ghosts and Skeletons
Begging for a treat
If we run out of candy will they pull a trick on us
Or is that custom dead like the great Stegosaurus?

THE PAPER TREE

I awoke on Saturday to see
A fully toilet papered tree
A friend of my big sister Sue
Was showing that his love was true

"This fad is getting out of hand !"
My father yelled ...."Tell your fan
To clean that dang mess up my noon
Or he'll be zooming to the moon !"

The moral of this short sweet tale
Is "Send your love notes through the mail !"

TYRANNOSAURUS REX

If I lived in the days of Tyrannosaurus Rex
I would have to hide.. to save my little neck
He's used to eating bigger things and I'm such a little squirt
But he just might decide to have me for dessert !

SPIDER & THE FLY

"Come into my parlor" said the flyder to the spy
I mean.. "Come into my parlor said the fidor to the pie"
I mean "Come into my parlor shaid the pidor to the sky"
Aw, to heck with what the spider said ...Goodbye !

I spoke to wise old owl at the Zoo
I told him my name and the owl said "Who ?"
I said "I'm Hushpuppy Cornpone", repeating what I'd said
And the owl said "Who?" ..now my face was turning red

I said "I thought you were wise !"
And I spelled out my name
But the owl just said "Who?" ..it was driving me insane

I guess I lost my temper and I shouted at that bird
"I'm HUSHPUPPY CORNPONE !.. and You are a Nerd !"
Then I turned and stalked away 'cause I was awful mad
And I heard the owl ask someone "Who was that lad ?"

THE POTENTATE

A Potentate and Nabob from two distant lands
Were greeted at the station by a Bagpiper Band
The Nabob was trumped 'cause the Potentate was greater
So he had to walk behind.. with all the pooper scrapers.

SANTA CLAUS

Every one loves Santa Claus when he sings HO HO HO
On Christmas Eve he's always there with sleighbells in the snow
Do you remember every name of all his eight reindeer ?
I'll bet you do and I do, too..at least I did last year.

Dasher, Prancer, Cupid, Dancer and I think one was Mose
Donder, Blitzen..who am I missin'..
The one with the red nose !

His name starts with an R, but I know it isn't Rex
Or Rob or Rick or Ronald or Reginald or Rhett
If you know the answer, please give me a clue
Yell out the name that I forgot and I'll be thanking you.

INSTRUCTION SHEET

To put together this great toy, all you need to do
Is fasten this gizmo with a one inch bolt and screw
Then take the watchamacallit
And attach the whats-its-name
Insert six tiny doohickeys
Inside the outer frame
Glue the thingamajig to parts A, B and C
Then bend the spring inside the widget
Twenty two degrees
You will need a crescent wrench, a stapler and some glue
A Phillips Head screwdriver and a boy scout hatchet, too
If you don't have the patience of a Saint
Take it back and tell the store an engineer you aint !

THE PIPERS SON

Tom, Tom…the Pipers son
Stole a pig and away he run
He taught the pig to yodel and dance
And sing "Louey, Louey" for the King of France.

OLD PROVERB

Early to bed, early to rise
Makes you healthy, wealthy and wise
But party all night and sleep till one
Sounds like ..a lot more fun.

BREAKFAST

When I eat my cereal it goes SNAP, CRACKLE, POP !
Such a noisy Breakfast I don't need
I wish that it would stop
When I put bananas on it..then blessed silence follows
Instead of SNAP, CRACKLE, POP !
It goes Mooosh, Slurp Slop, Swallow.

Jebediah Oink told his Ma and Pa
"People say I've got the greatest voice in Arkansas
I can make the rafters ring when I sing Opera songs
I feel it in my bones and that's where I belong

But folks here in the Ozarks
Didn't have that in mind
And they gave him a prize ..of a different kind
Yes, Jebediah Oink was destined for success
As first prize winner in the Hog Calling contest !

SNORE STORY

Henry Dowd snored so loud it woke up all his neighbors
They even wrote about it in the local daily papers
It was louder than a chain saw..sawing up pine logs
It was louder than a siren or a pack of hungry dogs
It was louder than a snowmobile at the crack of dawn
It was louder than a freight train or a Rock Band on your lawn
The could hear it in Milwaukee
The could hear it in St. Paul
They could hear it clear to China
Where it echoed off that wall
When Henry Dowd stopped snoring
They declared a Holiday
And his funeral brought smiles
As the hearse took him away.

FOOD FIGHT

"There's a worm in your spaghetti !
There's a fly in your soup !"
"Mom, make him stop it…he's ruining my food !
Now I'll have to inspect..every single bite I take
Brother, dear.. I just saw a bug
On the last spoonful <u>you</u> ate !"

I SCREAM

I scream, you scream, we all scream for ice cream
Eat it with chili dogs, sardines and baked beans
Moon pies, french fried, doughnuts and layer cake
And I'll have, you'll have, we'll all have a stomach ache.

RAGAMUFFIN

Don't throw away my raggedy shirt
It's still my favorite
And the sneakers with the holes in them
And the jeans that shrank a bit
It takes a while to break in clothes
Until they feel just right
And you won't get them away from me..
....At least without a fight.

CAPTAIN COOK

Who was the famous sea captain who sailed around the world ?
Aye, it was Captain Cook.. who discovered hula girls
I can't remember all they ate but when they went to dine
The cannibals ate Captain Cook and said he tasted fine.

CHRISTMAS

Is coming
The goose is getting fat
Please drop a penny
In the old mans hat
If your purse is empty
As you stroll the Boulevard
He'll gladly take your VISA
Or Mastercard.

BEWITCHED

All the Witches I have seen wear tall pointy hats
And ride on skinny broomsticks with spooky ol' black cats
They get good mileage on their brooms on Halloween
And it saves a lot of money on oil and gasoline.

I'D LIKE TO BE

When I grow up an Astronaut
Is what I'd like to be
Or maybe a Ship Captain
Who sails the seven seas
And you may laugh but I could be
The President and then
You can brag and say that
You knew me way back when!

THE MONSTER

They lock the Monster in this Dungeon every single night
The Monster's brain is not the same as that of you and I
When morning comes they let him out to stroll around the grounds
He likes to pick pink posies and smell Chrysanthemums.

They say he has the strength of ten so do not shake his hand
Just smile and say "Hello" to him.. and he will understand.

The Villagers once frightened him with torches in the night
They said "Kill, Kill the Monster… he's a horrid scary sight!"
But Igor Beavor found this Dungeon cell to put him in
And he feels safe inside where mobs can't get to him.

VENUS FLY TRAP

Once I was captured by a meat eating plant
It said "I will eat you."
I said "No you can't !"
"You are a Venus Fly Trap who eats flies and ants!"
And I finally got away.. but is ate up my pants !

ATTENTION SPAN

When I was in the second grade
My attention span
Was shorter than it takes
A Bumble Bee to land
But I can really concentrate since I'm 13
With a text book propped in front of
My Mad Magazine.

MY TEACHER

I brought an apple to my teacher every day this week
I said "Good morning Miss Penrod" before I took my seat
I sharpened all her pencils…and tidied up her desk
And every time she sneezed
        I made sure that she was blessed…..(Gesundheit !)
All my classmates tease me "Did you bring a rose bouquet ?"
But they forgot that report cards..are coming out today.

BUBBLE TROUBLE

Soap bubbles in my bathtub
Surround my rubber boats
I pretend that it's sea foam…and
Other stuff that floats
But some bubbles from my bottom
Go "POP ..POP..POP..POP"
And don't smell too good
When they come to the top.

TUXEDO JUNCTION

Mrs. Penguin told her Mister "It just isn't fair !"
"Your tuxedo's always on for any big affair
But poor me…. I don't have a single thing to wear
Please buy me a white fur coat like that polar bear."

VULGARIAN

An uncouth Vulgarian, resembling a baboon
Said "Fingers were invented before there was a spoon."
But when he went to eat his soup (I think it was split pea)
He used a bowl and spoon…and was couth as he could be.

MISSION BELLS

The bell ringer at the Mission
Stuffed fruitcake in his ears
So he wouldn't need a hearing aid
In his senior years.

KANGAROO MAIL

The Outback of Australia goes on and on and on
The farms are few and far between underneath the sun
But the mail must be delivered so the hardy Kangaroo
Makes sure that it's delivered to you and you and you

He has a built in pouch that's just right for letters
And the little 'Roo inside checks for stamp forgetters
If there is no stamp upon it, the little Kangaroo
Will write on the outside of the letter "Postage Due".

THE SEASONS

I love the summertime, after school is out
Play all day, rain or shine…run around and shout.

Wintertime brings snowflakes that fall all through the night
You wake up to a Magic World, a real kids delight.

Spring has wind for flying kites, way up in the sky
In June you lie there in the grass and watch the clouds roll by.

Fall has football games and bands and shadows grow so long
And yellow leaves dance in the wind all across the lawn.

All four seasons have some things that I look forward to
I'd miss a lot of fun if there were only one or two.

TERRIBLE BORNEO CURSE

This Hideous Idol from Borneo has a curse on it's head
Those who gaze upon it turn to stone, it is said
So BEWARE of opening this page of the book
Uh oh…how awful…too bad it you looked !

CABOOSE

"My caboose is loose" said the Choo Choo train
I better back up till it's on again
If I move ahead.. and let it go
It'll be a lunchwagon in a week or so
I lost one in Elyria..now it's a Caboosateria.

BIG ROCK STAR

I'm moving on the fast lane at Einstein Junior High
I never crack a book..so I'm just gettin' by
Why fill my brain with all that stuff that I don't really need
'Cause I'll be a big Rock Star as you can plainly see.

HUSH HUSH X-2 ROCKET

The Government is testing the Hush-Hush X2 rocket
The plans are so secret that they keep 'em in their pocket
They don't need computers so the cost is very low
Just light a match to the end and watch that critter go !
It leaves a trail of sparks and sparkles in the evening sky
And it should be great to celebrate 4th of July.

MARY'S LAMB

Mary had a little lamb that followed her to school
Teacher said "He can't come in 'cause it's against the rule"
The lamb said "I'll wait outside till they ring the bell"
But Mary brought him right inside during Show & Tell.

MY SHADOW

I raced my shadow around the block one morning at 9
At first he was ahead of me but then he fell behind
Before we hit the last turn..we were side by side
But he was out in front again at the finish line

Elmo said to race around the block the <u>other</u> way
Then I could beat my shadow and I said "Okay"
So late in the afternoon we raced the block and then..
My shadow was so fast that he beat me once again !

GOURMET

Some people like gourmet food in fancy restaurants
Smelly cheese and Vichyssoise and Chateaubriand
But it doesn't cost an arm and leg to please Michael Metski
The food he loves the most is just a hot dot and a Pepsi.

FLEA MARKET

I went to a flea market..but didn't buy a flea
They were too expensive for a poor soul like me
I guess all the rich folks will buy them for their cat
Or give them to a rich dog who has everything but that.

CANDY GRABBERS

A car full of Monsters and Punky People Eaters
Are off the grab the candy ..away from Trick or Treaters
Every October they appear on the scene
And try to ruin everybodys Haloween
Some wear false faces or dress in Ghost-like sheets
But some are <u>real</u> Monsters with long dagger teeth
BEWARE ! BEWARE !..They might be anywhere
And if they scare you bad enough you'll need clean underwear !

TURTLE & HARE RACE

A Hare raced a Turtle down Lucky Lane
(A Hare is a Rabbit...by another name)
It shouldn't have been close 'cause the Rabbit was faster
But lazy attitudes often spell disaster.

The Rabbit lollygagged..along the way
He even had a Sugar Doughnut at a café
Meanwhile the Turtle, with his own cheering crowd
Did not make a Pit Stop, although they were allowed.

The sponsors had signs on the Turtles' shell
Which covered his back to a fare thee well
But the track was too slow for most folks taste
'Cause it took two hours to finish the race.

Down the home stretch they came...the Rabbit on his knees
Laughing and teasing and shootin' the breeze
But he bumped his knee on a stone he hurdled
And he lost the race by the length of a Turtle.

LEAPING LIZARD

The Leaping Lizard is very rare
You just can't find them everywhere
On a colored quilt he blends right in
Like a little See-through Chameleon.
When he's loose around the house
You don't know where he's at
So tie a red ribbon on his tail
Or make him wear a hat.

BIRDWATCHER

We birdwatchers rise at dawn
And spyglass we take along
Hoping for a glimpse to catch
A Double Breasted Booby Hatch
Or a further look may reveal
A Silver Tinkled Glockenspiel.

WITCH DOCTOR

If you have a friend who's sick in bed
With a fever and a stuffy head
I'll tell my Witch Doctor in Trinidad
That your little friend feels awful bad.

The old Witch Doctor has Magic Powers
And waltzes with lizards in the midnight hours
He'll chant "Ooga Booga" in his Voodo hat
And your friend will get well..<u>just like that</u>!

GRAND UNIFORM

What a fine fitting uniform with Medals and Gold Braid
Undoubtedly a General..ready for parade
His brass buttons sparkle and his boots shine so bright
You can see your reflection as he steps into the night.

The many fine Medals that are there on his chest
Show that of the Generals he must be the best
Everyone obeys when he barks out commands
Like a tall Drum Major in the Queens marching band.

He toots for a Taxi…and then he toots some more
And a grander looking doorman never opened up a door.

MEXICOW

While traveling through Mexico
I saw a cow beside the road
Stuck in mud up to her knees
So we found a rope and pulled her free
Then I swear I heard her say to us…
MOOOOO chas Gracias !

THE ARTIST

I'm drawing a picture of my friend Mary Ann
I'm not a Rembrandt yet but I do what I can
She says "I don't like this and I don't like that !"
She thinks one eye is crooked and her cheeks are too fat
Her ears are too big and her nose is too red
But I didn't erase the picture…I erased her instead !

STATUE

A statue in the park of an Indiana town
Impressed all the visitors who
Walked around the grounds
The sign said "This fine General is
Marquis de Lafayette"
But the pigeons couldn't read
And so they pooped on it.

JACK AND THE GIANT

"Fee Fi Fo Fum !"...the Giant said to Jack
It nearly caused the little lad..to have a heart attack
Then the Giant found his dentures underneath his sweater
And said "Now that my teeth are in I can speak much better."

JACK SPRATT

Jack Spratt would eat no fat ..his wife would eat no lean
She's a round Butterball while he's a long Stringbean
Trimming fat from Pork Chops was not hard at all
But when it came to Hamburger it drove them up the wall
Nutritionally speaking, they both missed the boat
As all you kids reading this have learned by now, I hope.

BANG!
BOOM
Whizzzzz!
ZOOM!
Crash!
POP-POP
BLAM!

It sounds like a war outside
Just like No Mans Land
Those sounds we hear ring in our ears
But that's the price we pay
For celebrating July 4th..our Independence Day !

Me finger gehurtin

FINGER IN THE DIKE

A little Dutch boy ..many years ago
Was cheered by the Dutch as a great Hero
'Cause he stuck his finger in the dike
And kept the flood at bay all night.

So I went to Holland just last year
To find that lad who folks had cheered
He was old and gray and seemed confused
As he stood there in his wooden shoes
"Bring me a cork!" I heard him shout
"So I can pull my finger out."

71

On Halloween I think I'll make a special treat for you…
With bat wings and creepy things and cook then in a stew
Some purple catfish eyeballs and Toadstools a la mode…
And a black cat, squashed flat…that I found on the road.

Some rats tails and green toenails form a Witches feet
A moldy buzzard gizzard and a hunk of smelly cheese
A rat, a bone and a hank of hair with a Mummys Curse..
And a shrunken head, cold and dead..how could it be worse…

Some cobwebs from a spiders den, and to make sure I scare you…
I'll sprinkle salt all over me and I'll throw me in there, <u>too</u> !

AMOEBA

I have a pet amoeba…I take to school with me
He only has one cell so he's really hard to see
I put him in my lunchbox with a magnifying glass
'Cause if he's on my Twinkie..my lunch will be his last !

I ask for a doggie bag…every time I eat
I say it's for my dog…to give that pooch a treat
But I'm sure they know…by the look upon my face
It's really for myself…(though I give the dog a taste)

LONG MEMORY

The African elephant has enormous ears
But he never spreads gossip no matter what he hears
He has a trunk in front and he has a tail behind
So you wouldn't know which end is which, if you were blind
He's famous for his memory, for which he has been praised
So you may get a card from him...on your next birthday.

SUMMER RAIN

Looking out the window pane
All I see is RAIN RAIN RAIN
But that don't bother me at all
I get my raincoat from the hall
Bare feet sloshing down the street
Splashing puddles…ankle deep

I feel the rain upon my tongue
Now here comes the smiling sun
A rainbow's high up in the sky
A lovely world for you and I
Why do grown ups all complain
It's so much fun..the summer rain !

IZZY LAZYBONES

Little Izzy Lazybones looked for a place to nap
He said "I'll know a fine place in the park
I think that I'll try that !"
He crawled inside that canon..
So snug from the rain
And before you could say "Grover Cleveland"
Was snoozing once again.

It was on a well known Holiday
And people came to cheer
As they fired that big canon off
Like they did last year
The gun went BOOM and Izzy went ZOOM
Making history
So little Izzy isn't with us any more…is he ?

BELLY BUTTON

I have a belly button
But I don't know what it's for
I know I can't unbutton it
And there is one thing more
Does it have a function
For better or for worse
Or is it a decoration
Like an epaulette on shirts ?

77

CAMEL RIDE

A lady from Bangor, Maine
While riding a camel complained
This ride is too bumpy
The camel's too grumpy
So next time I'm taking a train !

12 DAYS OF CHRISTMAS

"On the 10th day of Christmas my true love gave to me
Ten Lords-a-Leaping on a small pear tree"
I think that song is way too long and just between us two
They really must have been ten frogs or I don't think it's true.

AH-ONE, AH-TWO

When Punjabi plays flute and the Cobra hears the sound
He doesn't know rock music from a hole in the ground
But he likes to swing and sway when Punjabi blows
And he probably was a big fan of the Lawrence Welk Show.

TARZAN

I swung from a grapevine like Tarzan of the Apes
I didn't swing far but I smashed a lot of grapes
I yelled AHHHHHHHOOOOOOOEEEEYYY !
Just like the Mighty One
Calling Tantor the elephant to come
But all that showed up was a cat and a dog
And a farmer who thought I was calling his hogs.

FOXY GRANDPA

Is Clark Kent..SUPERMAN ?
Did Elvis have a lot of fans ?
Does the sun shine? Is it dark at night ?
Are zebra stripes..black and white ?
Is the ocean wet? Do snowflakes fall?
Down South do they say you-all ?
If I ask Grandpa if he's feelin' good
He says "Does a bear poop in the woods ?"

FLOATER

Ben Franklin fell asleep out in the water
He didn't wake up for half and hour
He discovered when you're fat it's hard to drown
(Unless, of course, you're upside down)

MINARET

A Ghastly Ghoul from Istanbul popped from a Minaret
And rolled some Turk tobacco ..into a cigarette
I said "You will get cancer"…and this is what he said
"It won't hurt me at all 'cause I'm already dead !"

MARCHING BAND

I'd like to play the tuba
In the High School Band
And UMPAH UMPAH down the field
Marching by the stands
Brass buttons on my coat and sleeve
And gold braid on my hat
Those little flutes are mighty cute
But I want more than that.

Or I could bang while cymbols clang
On the big bass drum
BOOM BOOM.. CLANG CLANG
BOOM BANG.. BLUM !
Until I get to High School
I'll practice in my room
And I hope that Dad doesn't mind the

Boom blam
Boom !

GRUMPTH BUMPTH

The dentist gave me Novacaine
And said that I
Will feel no pain
My tongue got thick and my lips wouldn't work
When he asked me a question I said
"Grumpth..bumpth.. thurg "

MOCKING BIRD

A mocking bird mocked Skyler Nerd
Echoing his every word
"I'm Skyler"..said Skyler Nerd
"I'm Skyler"…mocked the bird
"Stop that !" said Skyler Nerd
"Stop that !" said the bird

"You're a Nincompoop!" said Skyler Nerd
"You're a Double Nincompoop !" said the bird
Skyler got so mad that he barfed his dinner
But the bird just laughed
And flew south for the winter.

RUN FOR THE ROSES

My Uncle has a race horse
Who always comes in last
Though his Daddy was a Champion
Because he was so fast
No matter how Jockey Jimbo tries to urge him on
He stops to smell the roses on the race track lawn.

CHORUS
Oh, Stumblebum Moses, son of Mensch of War
You look like a Champion but you don't ever score
You'll never win a race if you stop to smell the flowers
And getting to the finish line can take a half an hour.

On the day of the Derby at 100 to one
Was Stumblebum Moses with Jockey Jimbo on
He whispered in his ear that "the winner wears a wreath
With hundreds of roses and another for your teeth."

Well, those were Magic Words for Stumblebum Moses
And he won by the nose that loved to smell the roses !

REPEAT CHORUS

BEDTIME STORY

Read me that story one more time
About the rabbit and the porcupine
And Pogo-rumble-popple-weird
The dwarf who had a ten foot beard
And Cinderellas' wicked Stepsisters
Made her wear rags and hand-me-down slippers
If I've mixed these storys, for heavens sake
It's because I'm too sleepy to..stay…awake
……..ZZZZZZZZZZZZZZZ

COLORS

I have a box of crayons
Aunt Birdie gave to me
But I ran out of paper..so sooner or later
I started in coloring ME
I colored my nose and each of my toes
Green, yellow, purple and blue
And when I'm through with coloring me
I'll start in COLORING YOU

WILD BILL HICCUP

Wild Bill Hiccup was the best
Chasing outlaws way out West
He was hired to keep the peace
In the town of Gooberpeas

Yes, Sheriff Hiccup was the law
But he was cursed with one slight flaw
He hiccuped often when he spoke
So the outlaws laughed and joked

The outlaws said "Just count to three !
Then we'll draw out pistols free."
Wild Bill said "One, Two (hiccup) Three!"
And his bullets missed and hit a tree
(But a limb fell off on those badmen
And Wild Bill had won again !)

HAIRCUT

I went to get a haircut…in the barber chair
I said "I want to look so cool and debonair
Put some bangs in front and shape it like a bowl
Just like the third stooge…in Larry, Curly, Moe."

FISHING WORMS

Creepy, crawly, fishing worms
Put them in a can
Squishy, squashy, slimy creatures
Crawling on your hand
Pink and brownish sand colored
Slithery and damp
Just like live spagetti
But much more wriggly than.
Take them on your fishing trip
Where they can be the host
To fish they are delicious
But their taste buds are
So gross.

HIGH SOCIETY

"I'm Mrs. Wigglebottom…I'm as grown up as can be "
"I'm Mrs. Pansypotter…would you like a cup of tea ?"
"My, what pretty shoes you have…aren't they, Mrs. Cat?"
"They cost two hundred dollars…and a hundred for my hat"

"I'm just about to pour…does Mrs. Cat drink tea ?"
"Mrs. Cat says meow…which means milk for me."
"Have you heard the latest gossip going 'round ?
That naughty Mrs. Tattletale was grounded by her Mom."

Thanks for the tea and cookies..I better go on home
Before my Mom reports her pearls are missing on the phone."

BATES MOTEL

Would I ever stop at the Bates Motel..?
You can bet I won't
The person in that swivel chair..
Is just a bag of bones..
That scary scene still haunts my dreams
Just like a Ghoulish play..
Reminding me to send a nice card
Every Mothers day.

AMNESIA

I sometimes forget things
Especially whats-his-name
He lives way out in the woods,
I think it is in Maine
I tied a string around my finger
Hoping it would help
But the person it reminds me of is
Somebody else.

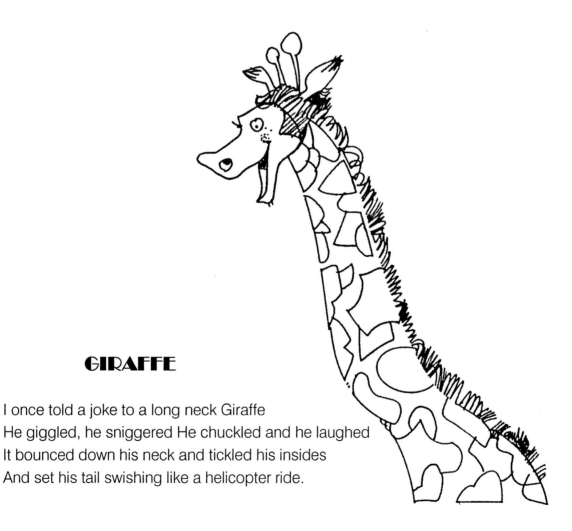

GIRAFFE

I once told a joke to a long neck Giraffe
He giggled, he sniggered He chuckled and he laughed
It bounced down his neck and tickled his insides
And set his tail swishing like a helicopter ride.

SCARY SPIDER

Little Miss Muffit sat on her tuffit
Eating some curds and whey
(That's really cottage cheese..
Said in the old time way)
Anyway, a spider sat down beside her
And scared her, so they say
And spiders still have that effect
On many folks today.

MR LINCOLN

"Are your legs too long, Mr. Lincoln ?
I'd say you're the tallest man around."
He said "They're just a perfect fit
'Cause when you think of it
They're just long enough to reach the
ground."

92

THE FLY

There's a fly on your nose
Oh there it goes
Now it's back on your clothes
Brush it off but It comes right back
I'll give that bugger a solid whack!
I missed him once and once again
He's faster than greased lightning
Shoo fly…you little pest
Get the heck off my chest !
Now he's on my popsicle
Now on my neck…does that tickle !
That pesky fly is driving me mad
When I whack him he's gonna be dead
Oh, there's a fly swatter over there
Settin' on the kitchen chair
Now I've got it so fly beware !
What's that ?…He's gone !

THE FROG

Higglety.. pigglety.. jugglety jog
I'll give you a penny to borrow your frog
I'll put him in the Reptile Race
With leaping lizards and toads and snakes
If he wins.. he'll get a prize
Maybe a dollar, maybe five
I'll give you one half ..'cause I'm no hog
I mean half the money, not half the frog.

KNIGHTS

One Knight told the other "I got caught in the rain..
It rusted my joints so I have to use a cane
In fact, the only thing I can move is my mouth
Have you got a can opener ..so I can get out ?"

COUNTING SHEEP

I'm counting sheep to go to sleep
When I go to bed
There goes a green one, there's a blue one
That ones orange and red
"Silly girl !" My sister says
"Sheep are black or white..
Every picture in the books
Prove that I am right"
My friend Betsy says so too
And so does he brother
Well let them dream in black and white
I choose to dream in **COLOR** !

TV STATION W.O.W.

Meriweather Cloudburst, the blonde weather lady
Says "It will rain tonight….probably….well, maybe
   There's a cold front in the North
   There's a warm front in the South
   Raindrops ruin your hairdo
   So get your umbrellas out."
There's only a 50/50 chance the forecast will be right
But pretty Meriweather makes us tune in every night !

BUBBLE GUM

In our Bubblegum blowing contest…
The boys against the girls
I blew the biggest bubble
Seen in all the world
I huffed & puffed and huffed & puffed
Till the very end
And it could have been much bigger
But I ran out of wind.

LION TAMER

The Lion Tamer, Waldo.. is brave as he can be
He puts lions through hoops of fire every day at 3
The final act he puts his head into the lions mouth
And a hush falls on the crowd until he pulls it out
Waldo says what bothers him is not the fear of death
But Leo the lion has such awful stinky breath.

LESTER BROWN

Lester Fester Leroy Brown
Writes and draws things upside down
If you want to see what Lester said
You'll have to stand upon your head.

ALLIGATOR / CROCODILE

The alligator's not exactly like the crocodile
One has a skinny nose…and slobbers when he smiles
Their skin is rough as cobblestone…and if you're caught between
You'll see the biggest food fight…that you have ever seen !

GRAND OPERA

I went to see an opera….by a guy named Wolfgang
Some of them held spears…while the rest of them sang
One guy sang in a high voice..another way down low
And some dancers in their underwear danced on tippy toe

The songs were in French, I think or maybe it was Russian
And their faces were all painted or maybe they were blushin'
They raised their swords and shouted and the King wore a crown
Then the fat lady sang…and the curtain came down.

SISTERS POEM

My sister had a favorite poem that everybody knows
She loved to recite it..and this is how it goes:
    "Sugar and Spice and everything nice.
    That's what little girls are made of.
    Frogs and snails and puppydog tails.
    That's what little boys are made of."

But now that she is thirteen she's changed her mind I guess
Boys are all she talks about and which ones she likes best
I said "Ho Ho, big sister! You've changed your mind I see."
She said that poem is still true for little pests like me.

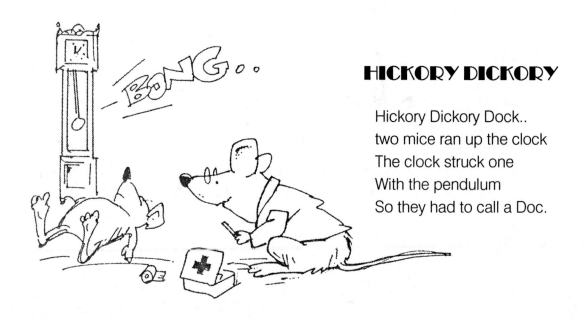

HICKORY DICKORY

Hickory Dickory Dock..
two mice ran up the clock
The clock struck one
With the pendulum
So they had to call a Doc.

MY DREAMS

A Tiger on ice skates..making figure eights
A Lion in pajamas reading the sport page
A bird who speaks in French or Greek..a poet Pelican
(Whose beak, says Ogden Nash, holds more than his belly can)
Look anywhere around the world…you won't find these things
But I have seen them many times..in my dreams !

TREE CARVER

I carved a heart in a tree for my love Mary Lou
But her name was too long so I just carved "I love You"
Sad to say she moved away so I told my new love Sue
"Come see the heart I carved especially for you"
There's a lesson for you Romeos when on a tree you start
Make it generic when you carve a heart.

THE THING

What the heck is that…that landed on your hat !
With eyes like a rattlesnake and wings like a bat
It's hideous beyond belief, you'll have to take my word
Don't move or make it angry for landing on a nerd.

MONEY MACHINE

I invented a Magical Money Machine
You put in gumballs and green Jellybeans
And out pops pennies, nickles and dimes
To put in your Piggybank one at a time.

FLY AND THE FROG

A fly and frog were on a log
The fly said "I hate frogs !"
"You smell like a skunk if I'm not mistaken"
And the frog zapped out his tongue
And ate him.

TOOTH FAIRY

When I lost my front tooth ..the Tooth Fairy came
And left me Two dollars…a pretty fair exchange
Tomorrow I'll leave Grandpas dentures there instead
And I'll be a rich kid..when I get outa bed.

104

HOUSE RULES

Mind your manners, Reginald Brown
Whenever company comes to town
Wash your hands and comb your hair
Say "Yes, Ma'am" and say "Yes Sir"
Don't reach over and grab the peas
Say "Will you pass the biscuits, please?"
Use your fork…not your hands
And don't dribble ketchup on your chin
Don't talk with your mouth full of food
Everyone knows that's very rude
Don't slurp soup with a zoop, zoop noise
That's the do's and don'ts for girls and boys
When the company's gone away
You can go back to your old slob ways.

THE ARROW

I shot an arrow into the air
It fell to earth I know not where
But somewhere in this land, I'll bet
There's an arrow through
Somebody's hat.

MY CAT

I learned to read with the "Cat in the Hat"
It made me a reader and I'm thankful for that
So I wrote a story about my cat
Who was too fat to fit in a hat

Then I gave my cat a grocery sack
And he jumped inside.. flippity flap
It's his favorite thing when he wants to play
Cats are really funny that way.

MONACLE

I went to the Monacle Mart
To buy me a Monacle..so I'd look smart
Just like the Red Baron…up in the sky
But I can't keep the darn thing in my eye.

THE PRINCESS AND THE FROG

A Princess in a Castle Grand
Was searching for her real dream man
"A dashing prince is what I need
To sweep me off my Royal feet.
My trusty servants, go forth please
And find and bring one back to me !"

One Prince they brought had two left feet
"A lousy dancer, no doubt" said she
Another was so round and fat
"Nay, nay !" she said "I don't want that"

Then a frog hopped in with a tale to tell
"I'm a young Prince under a Magic Spell.
Just kiss my lips and you will see
Behold !....a dashing Prince for thee !"

The Princess said "Alas, I'll try"
But the Magic seemed to go awry
She kissed the Prince when they were wed
And she turned into a frog instead !

"Eat your spinach. It will put color in your cheeks!"
"Who wants green cheeks?"

"How do you get down off a duck ?"
"The same way you got on, Silly."

"Is it true that a charging bear will not hurt you
if you carry a flashlight ?"
"Yes. If you carry it fast enough."

"Where should they make smokers eat ?"
"In a Coughateria."

"Could George Washington throw a silver dollar
across the Potomac River if he were alive today?"
"No. A dollar doesn't go as far as it used to."

"Teacher says I need an encyclopedia."
"Nonsense. You'll walk to school like everybody else."

"I just had pancakes and snu for breakfast."
"What's snu ?"
"Not much. What's new with you?"

"My Uncles cattle ranch out west is called the
Lazy J Circle Q ABCD Bar XYZKPYN."
"How big is the herd?"
"Very small. Not many survive the branding."

"My pet frog died. How deep should I bury it ?"
"KNEE DEEP ! KNEEDEEP !"

"I think I've got amnesia."
"How long have you had it?"
"Had what?"

"How can you make salt taste better ?"
"Sprinkle hamburger on it."

"If most cats have 9 lives what you call a cat with 8 ?"
"An Octopuss."

"Are some kids afraid of Santa Claus ?"
"Yes. The ones with claustraphobia."

"What is gray and has 4 legs and a trunk?"
"A mouse on vacation."

SILLY WILLY

Silly Willie Piccadilly
Counted up his toes
Before he went to bed each night
then he'd blow his nose…
"I know I just can't fall asleep
Silly Willie said…
"If one of them is missing
And has rolled beneath my bed."

POLAR BEAR

People think that Polar Bears love the ice and snow
That' it's their fondest wish to fish at 35 below
But when the Polar bear retires
  He takes a plane and flies..
    To the sunny shores of Florida
      Even as you and I.

KARATE KID

I'm the Karate Kid...I'm tough as can be
I say HAYUPHH ! and I kick my feet
If you mess with me you'll pay the Piper
(But I'm really a hugger ♥ instead of a fighter)

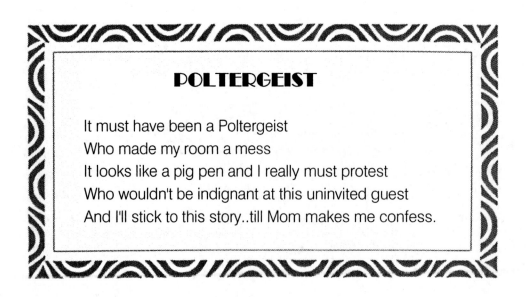

POLTERGEIST

It must have been a Poltergeist
Who made my room a mess
It looks like a pig pen and I really must protest
Who wouldn't be indignant at this uninvited guest
And I'll stick to this story..till Mom makes me confess.

MAN WITH 2 HEADS

The man with two heads is almost like a twin
He can see where he's going and see where he's been
One head can sleep while the other's wide awake
And two heads blow out candles better on a Birthday Cake

One head can watch his coat while the other eats his lunch
'Cause purse thieves are lurking.. in many restaurants
One thing about two heads I've save 'cause it's the best
If he loses one of them..he'll still have one head left !

If privacy is what you seek..and there are those who'd take a peek
Make a copy for your door and you won't be bothered anymore !

Use your markers to color this critter
And you might even scare the babysitter

A BOOK OF ME

I'm writing a book about me
A best seller it may be
True adventures, big daydreams
Or just Tomfoolery ?

Like when I was almost three
And the cannibals captured me
When out of the jungle
My long lost Uncle
Came to set me free.

Then me and my best friend Joel
Rode a dog sled to the North Pole
It was way below zero
But we were heros
And never complained of the cold.

And when I was a Star in a Movie
The autograph seekers pursued me
But I hadn't learned to write my name
So they all got mad and booed me

Yes my life's had ups and downs
A hero one day..then a clown
But "That's life" as all us writers say
And it keeps our feet on the ground.

THIS
IS

THE END

Printed in the United States
2430

9 780759 613850